HOW TO RAISE A WILD CHILD

The Essential Guide to Raising Children Morally

By

Maia Collins

COPYRIGHT PAGE

Chapter 1

Introduction

The fate of a person is his character and moral guidelines by which he follows. The value system of each person largely depends on his upbringing, first of all, upbringing in the family.

The moral development of the child begins from an early age. Reaching adolescence is not a reason to let everything go by itself, justifying that the child has matured.

A teenager torn by contradictions is even more in need of moral guidelines, he needs to continue to be educated, but this will have to be done more tactfully than a few years earlier.

Chapter 2

How do children make moral choices?

One of the most difficult educational questions is how to teach children the difference between good and evil. This is mainly because parents are regarded as role models and must set an example that the offspring can follow. Before they can show their children the difference between good and evil, however, they must understand how their children make moral choices.

Until recently, it was believed that younger children were unable to make moral judgments. because they cannot recognize certain factors, such as a firm intention. **But research has shown that children can judge the difference between good and evil much better than previously thought.**

In the 1930s, Swiss psychologist Jean Piaget, known for his theory of cognitive development, explained **that children go through three stages of moral thought as they mature.** Psychologists who followed him have also studied how moral development proceeds and how children think about right and wrong.

To study moral judgment, Piaget presented the children with short stories and then asked them about them. Piaget applied her answers to different scenarios and also included morality in his consideration. From the findings, he concluded **that children are not able to take into account a person's intention when making moral decisions.**

Instead, they focus only on the actual circumstances.

Decades later, psychologist Lawrence Kohlberg developed his theory of moral development. He introduced children to moral predicaments to determine how they think about good and evil. **According to Kohlberg, the moral choices of children ages 2–10 are closely related to the** punishments **and** rewards **that come with them.** If an act is punished, then it is bad. If it is rewarded, it is good. However, the answer to how children choose between good and evil is not black or white.

Chapter 3

Are intentions important for children?

Do children not consider intent? Recent studies show that Kohlberg's and Piaget's theories of moral development are incomplete.

More recent studies show that children do include intent in their judgment, especially when the researchers help the children better understand the situation through pictures and toys.

However, children have a hard time remembering details, so it's especially important to specifically highlight an intention. **If they are not told that there may be an intention behind a person's action, they will therefore make their judgment solely based on the result** – as previous work has already suggested.

But to what extent are intentions and outcomes important for children? **Research on children and adults shows that the assessment of an intention can change depending on the outcome of the action.** Our opinion of other people's intentions depends on whether we rate the outcome of the action as good or bad, at all ages: if an action turns out badly, then both children and adults think that the intention behind it must have been bad. In principle, this also applies to actions with a positive result but is less pronounced.

Right and wrong with indirect consequences

Why are children and adults so quick to condemn an action perceived as bad, but are more reluctant to evaluate commendable actions? One possible answer is related to the violation of norms. The philosopher Richard Holton said **that our intuition about other people's intentions is based on whether the action violates or adheres to a norm.** If someone violates a set norm, then we assume that this action was intended. We think that people follow norms without much effort, but act consciously when they violate them.

This is also known as the Knobe effect. This describes the tendency **to judge the bad side effects of an action as intentionally induced, but the positive consequences of an action as not intentionally induced.**

Chapter 4

How children make moral choices

Recent studies show **that children's moral thinking is more complex than we had previously assumed.** The first studies that used moral dilemmas were very complex and therefore extremely difficult to interpret. In addition, the researchers at that time understood the cognitive abilities of children less well than we do today.

Recent studies show **that children's moral thinking is more complex than we had previously assumed.** The first studies that used moral dilemmas were very complex and therefore extremely difficult to interpret. In addition, the researchers at that time understood the cognitive abilities of children less well than we do today.

What values should be developed in children?

Moral education involves the formation of a certain system of values. These values are enduring, universal and are well known to most adults, even if they themselves consider something else valuable. Let's list some of these qualities:

responsibility;

a sense of duty;

patriotism;

conscience and honor;

the ability to distinguish between good and bad, good and evil;

willingness to overcome life's adversities;

mercy and sympathy, kindness;

patience and tolerance;

the ability to love.

Moral education involves the formation of these qualities.

What are the best parenting methods to use?

The main methods of moral education are also well known to everyone, but it is worth listing them with an adjustment for the adolescent age of the pupil.

Conversation. Do not confuse this method with moralizing. Reading notations in adolescents causes rejection and protest. Conversations should be based on discussion, analysis of life or literary examples, films. You can recall incidents from your life, exchange opinions about the film you watched, the transfer, trying to direct the thoughts of a teenager in the right direction. Frequent communication with highly moral people will bear fruit, even if their topic is the most ordinary things. Therefore, you need to communicate as much as possible with a teenager and try to surround him with people with high moral qualities.

Situational method. At a younger age, its manifestation is a game, when game situations are created in which the child has to make a decision. Teenagers also play, and some computer games are built in such a way that the hero has to make a moral choice. But still, for a teenager, you need to create a situation of choice in reality. To figure out what they will be is the task of parents. For example, a teenager may be faced with a choice whether to visit a big grandmother or go with friends to nature, whether to go to a disco or walk and feed the dog. Each correct decision in such situations is a brick from which the moral image of a person is built.

Punishment and encouragement. Punishing a teenager is dangerous, but sometimes necessary, but still in ordinary situations it is better to replace punishment with censure - for a child who already has certain moral guidelines in his soul since childhood, pangs of conscience are worse than deprivation of sweets. It is equally important to praise your child for good deeds and achievements.

Example. At all, the times of example is the most effective method of forming moral qualities. You can talk as much as you like about the fact that the elders need to be respected, but if you insult your parents at least once in front of the child, he will treat them, and then in you, disrespectfully. The older the child becomes, the greater the role played by the example, first of all, the lifestyle of his parents.

Based on these methods, it is necessary to build an educational process in the family, not forgetting that education is a continuous process, and not an episodic lecture.

Show an example

In pedagogy, there are three main stages of moral education.

Responsiveness. This quality is formed in children from early childhood, but even if time is lost, it is necessary to start with this. Teach him to take care of those who are close to him, whom he loves: about a younger brother or sister, about a grandparent, about parents when they are sick, about pets. Don't forget to do what you think a teenager should do.

The desire not to cause harm, which in the future should develop into a desire to do good deeds. The main methods here are conversation and personal example.

Understanding that it is not necessary to reason about the good, it must be created. It is not enough to understand what is good and what is bad, it is important to act morally. At this stage, you use your own example and situational method.

From the foregoing, it can be seen that the example is the most important and universal method of education.

What problems can parents face?

In their quest to cultivate moral qualities in a teenager, parents will inevitably face two problems.

The first is a negative influence from the outside. Parents will not be able to completely protect a teenager from the flow of negative information, but they should try to do it. The difficulty is that this should not deprive a growing person of the right to choose and make decisions. An additional tool that will help level the harm is a conversation. After discussing dubious information with your child, you will help him to adequately perceive it.

The second problem is that the most effective method of forming moral qualities is the example of parents. Therefore, you will have to start with self-education, and it is very difficult to recognize the need and begin to change.

But still, if parents have formed a desire to raise their child as a highly moral person, they will overcome these obstacles.

Chapter 5

How to raise your child to be a good person

How can you help your child become more like you? How do you educate him to be a morally good person? This requires more than a book about morality or stand timpani. 10 tricks on how children learn ethical decency.

If you want your child to be musical, let him learn an instrument. If you want to promote the sporting achievements of your child, send him to a sports club. And if you want to have an intelligent child, you support your reading pleasure and curiosity.

But how to teach ethics to a child? Moral ideas and good action? With a stand timpani alone, the topic is not off the table. However, it is again not rocket science to teach the offspring how a good person has to act.

1. Act the way you want your child to act

Act only according to the maxim by which you can at the same time wants it to become a general law. This instruction is a good start to serve as a good role model for your own little one.

Children look at the behavior of their parents. It affects them even more than verbal advice and instructions from mom and dad. So the first step to making your child a morally good person is pretty simple: just act morally well yourself.

2. Consistently set standards on what is right and what is wrong

What is right, what is wrong? To think in these categories and to classify things correctly, a child must first learn. And who better to teach the little ones than the parents themselves?

Above all, the consequence is important. Anyone who tells his children to only walk over green lights, but always scurries over red with the child in stressful everyday life confuses the child. It is better to get the offspring used to the norm before confronting them with exceptions.

3. Empower your child when they do well

If the child acts well on its own – for example, comforts the injured sister or hugs the grieving grandmother – the parents have to praise, praise, and praise! People – especially children – learn more through praise than through punishment.

If the child combines his good behavior with the praise of the parents, he internalizes these good deeds. In this way, they become the norm in his everyday life.

4. Explain to the child the reasons for (moral) rules

Thou shalt not slap, lie, steal: the list of what children should refrain from is long. However, this authoritarian announcement alone is not enough to put children on the right path.

Children want to understand things. You want to know the reasons why something is forbidden. A "You must not hit because it hurts the other child" is much more likely to follow a child than merely the request not to hit

5. Focus your child's attention on the feelings of others

Empathy is the key to morally good actions. If a child learns to interpret the feelings of his fellow human beings and build compassion, he will be less inclined to do evil to other people.

To learn empathy, it is enough for mom and dad to focus their child's attention on other people's feelings. Phrases like "Look, this boy hurt himself and is crying" train compassion.

6. Talk to your child about the importance of kindness

What's the point of being friendly? If you are kind to someone, it is likely that this person reflects the behavior and is also nice. If you are friendly, you sow peace instead of war.

There are many reasons for kindness. Explaining them to your children is the first step in turning them into friendly people.

7. Show your disapproval of unacceptable behavior

Morally correct behavior also includes knowing what's *wrong*. If you observe immoral behavior or even a violation of the law with your child, you should not sweep this under the carpet as a parent under any circumstances.

Addressing is always better than concealing. Only in this way does the child learn what is reprehensible and why.

8. Increase your child's awareness of good choices

Parents are usually aware that communication plays a major role in upbringing. It is best to help children make decisions and give them useful advice.

If, for example, the child can decide for himself whether to give one of his two chocolate chips to his little brother, you can steer him in the right direction: "Look, you have two pieces. Would you like to give your brother some of them? Otherwise he's sad if he doesn't get one."

9. Emphasize fairness in games

Justice is a mainstay of moral action. How do you teach this feeling to your child? Quite simply: while playing!

If you *don't get angry with Mensche Dich*, *Uno* and Co. look very closely, you can give your child a lot for life. What is fair?

How does injustice feel? Why is fairness important at all? When playing, children learn faster – and of course easily!

10. Show enthusiasm for moral role models and achievements

Just as important as the disapproval of immoral behavior (see point 7) is the appreciation of desirable behavior.

If you observe exemplary behavior with the child – be it in real life or in Disney films – you can certainly explain it to the child. Even toddlers often

understand more than we trust
them to do.

The End